NO BOZOS!

By Randall D. Schultz
Illustrations by Bob Myers

PRICE/STERN/SLOAN
Publishers, Inc., Los Angeles
1984

Many thanks to the bozos and bozoettes
who made this book possible.

You know who you are.

On Becoming a Bozo:
An Introduction

It happens slowly. The first symptoms are almost unnoticeable.

Once in a while, you spend an entire afternoon watching golf on TV. You wear white athletic socks, even when you aren't pretending to exercise. You regularly take two spaces in crowded parking lots, and feel no pangs of guilt.

Then the process begins to accelerate.

You worry about foot odor, and begin to use foot deodorant faithfully.

You buy everything that's advertised on TV for $29.95 or less.

You invite insurance agents to your house for dinner.

Some of your old friends now avoid you. They say you've changed. You don't know what they're talking about. And, still, the process continues.

You give your waterbed to the hippies down the street. You now realize that if man were meant to sleep on water, he'd have rubber skin and fins.

You begin to hang out in donut shops, telling lies to total strangers about your incredible sex life.

You develop an unhealthy love for the feel of polyester against your skin.

You are becoming a bozo.

No, it's not pretty, but it's becoming more common every day. This year, bozoity —that which causes one to become a bozo —will affect more people than the common cold.

Bozoity is called "the silent crippler" for good reason. Blue Cross doesn't cover it. Neither does Medicare. Yet its effects can be found everywhere. In fact, the president of the company you now work for probably suffers from it.

This book is dedicated to all of the bozos in the world. May they one day realize that there is more to life than charter membership in the Barry Manilow Fan Club and family picnics in the backyard bombshelter. May they one day realize that they don't have to be bozos if they choose not to be.

But this book is really written for *you*, the non-bozo. It is you who must drag yourself out of bed every morning, knowing that somehow, somewhere, some bozo is going to do his best to ruin your day.

So study this book carefully. Avoid bozoity whenever possible. Beware of bozos.

But be kind, and tolerant. None of us is totally immune to bozoity. We all do bozoic things now and then. Deep down inside, we all have a little bozo lurking in the depths, just waiting to waddle out.

1
What is a Bozo?

Back in the old days, the only bozo you ever knew about was the clown on TV.

Now things are different. Everywhere you go, there are bozos.

They crowd the aisles of low-rent discount stores, fighting over half-price underwear whenever the word "SALE" appears in the window.

They wander the streets, listening to the Bee Gees on cheap imitation Walkmans, and try to walk like John Travolta.

They hang out in all-night coffee shops, making bets on who can drink the most coffee without going to the bathroom.

They scour garage sales looking for hidden treasures and genuine works of art that can be had for a quarter.

Bozos and bozoettes (females afflicted with bozoity) are fond of large singles' apartment buildings, where they try to lure members of the opposite sex onto their rented furniture and spend time talking about their divorces.

Bozos line up at the polls every four years to elect one of their own to the White House. (Bozos are the reason it takes so long to vote. They forget their sample ballots and have to decide who to vote for inside the little booth.)

Even in places which once served as havens for non-bozos—like out-of-the-way theatres which show artsy foreign films—bozos can now be found.

But what, exactly, is a bozo? Webster's Dictionary, (a few years behind as always), defines a bozo as a "fellow, guy." To truly understand what a bozo is, however, requires a much more detailed description.

Here's how Dr. Ralph Bozotros, the world's first and premiere Bozologist, describes a bozo in his treatise, "The Red Rubber Nose":

A bozo is a peculiar sort of fellow, who seems especially suited for life in our modern world. Bozos are apt to miss the meaning of the entire event because they are caught up in the meaningless details. A bozo will miss a fabulous sunset to rush off to put a few more coins in a parking meter when there's still 45 minutes left.

It seems the word "bozo" stems from the same Latin root ("bosa") as the word "boss." "Boss" originally meant "the bozo in charge."

Although the word has only recently become part of the common vocabulary, "bozo" was apparently first used to describe the Town Manager of Pompeii. It was he who selected the site for the city, next to a volcano which was, in his words, "colder than your mama." Unfortunately, history does not record the name of this pioneer bozo.

Bozos can be great people (on occasion), however, and we all have a few stashed away somewhere in our family trees. They're usually weird uncles who tell stupid jokes and wear funny-nose glasses at family reunions.

What separates bozos from nerds (the bookish, horn-rimmed intellectuals who are now making fortunes in computer programming) is the fact that bozos are found in virtually all segments of society. It is their growing numbers that make them so devastating to the non-bozo population.

Bozos are full of contradictions. They may be obsessed with personal hygiene, yet carry the same Kleenex around for 37 years. They tend to resist change, especially when it comes to changing their underwear. But because of their undue respect for authority, they might change their minds on an important political issue overnight—if their favorite bozo politician has just done so.

Many bozos are consumed by fears and worries. For example, during the Great Tylenol Panic of 1982, the Garden Variety Working Bozo dumped several bottles of the extra-strength capsules down his garbage disposal. Three years before he had bought a dozen bottles at a K-Mart "blue light special." He had taken hundreds of the capsules—but now he didn't want to risk it.

Of course, the poor bozo couldn't sleep for weeks thereafter. He had always taken two capsules before going to bed, to be sure he wouldn't wake up the next morning with a headache. Now his routine was broken, and he spent each night tossing and turning, wondering what he would do if he ever got another headache.

Most bozos fear **showing up late**. They wear digital watches (that either play music or tiny versions of video games) and refer to them constantly.

Bozoettes have an entire set of personal care fears, which include **being seen in public with my bra strap/girdle/false eyelash glue/panty line showing**.

Bozos dress funny. They wear colors that don't go together, and try to mix stripes, polka-dots, and patterns in the same outfit. Often they look like walking patchwork quilts.

Dr. Bozotros estimates that as many as one person in three is a certifiable bozo. Not to worry, though. A bozo of today can be a non-bozo tomorrow, just by increasing his bozo consciousness and avoiding things like Presto logs, individually wrapped slices of cheese, Pam, plastic furniture, and synthetic fabrics in colors not found in nature.

Take the good doctor's advice: Study bozos. See how they act, where they work, what they like to do, what they wear.

Then do the opposite.

The Seven Warning Signs of Bozoity

1. Inflammation and swelling of the proboscis.

2. Dramatic change in sense of humor.

3. Feelings of physical attraction toward Bob Barker or Eve Arden.

4. Habitual scratching of mosquito bites until they bleed.

5. An intense desire to do algebra problems.

6. Constant voicing of opinions on matters of little or no significance.

7. Not knowing the other six signs of bozoity.

2
Where Bozos Roam

Once you start noticing them, it seems as though bozos are everywhere. You can always find bozos in the supermarket. They wait in the "10 items or less" lines, trying to sneak through with at least 15. They will also try to pay by check in the "cash only" lines, pretending they didn't see the sign.

At the gas station, they always pull up to the wrong side of the pump, and then try to stretch the hose to reach the gas tank. The hose is always a foot short, so they have to get back into their cars and move a little closer. This takes an extra ten minutes, and only happens when you're already late.

There are places you can go to avoid bozos—but not many. You could go for a hike in the mountains, or lock yourself in the bathroom. A hot air balloon ride or a sky-diving jump would be a good way to spend some time away from bozos. You can go to a movie theatre showing a Monty Python film and be sure of sitting with more non-bozos than bozos.

A trip to the South Seas would be a great place to escape from bozos, as long as you didn't go with a tour group, or plan to stay at a Club Med.

The moon is always free of bozos.* So is a cemetery (unless you don't want to be around dead bozos, either).

If you're getting the idea that the best way to avoid bozos is to be alone or with a small group of your friends, then you're beginning to catch on.

There are times when you don't mind being around bozos. Your bozo tolerance is high, and you feel like doing something bozoic, or being with people you can laugh at.

When you're in such a mood, you can always go bowling or miniature golfing.

*Except for a few brief interludes during the Seventies.

13

Young bozos and bozoettes love to play miniature golf, although most bozologists are still baffled when it comes to explaining why. Perhaps it has something to do with hitting colored balls.

Discos are full of bozos.

Bozos love to shop at "dime" stores. If you want to watch a mega-bozo in action, wait by the coin-operated photo booth. The m.b. is the guy inside, attempting a seductive pose.

Bozos like to kill time in places that don't charge admission. You see lots of them in enclosed shopping malls, eating ice cream cones as they wander aimlessly from store to store. They ignore "No Eating" signs, and drop big, mushy scoops of rocky road on the carpet, in which, inevitably, you step.

Bus stations are full of bozos, who like to ride in buses and spend a great deal of time asking the bus driver stupid questions. Most bus-riding bozos feel that if man were meant to fly, he would have been given wings. If you ask them why man doesn't have steel belted radials instead of feet, they look at you like you're some kind of bozo.

Once in a while you might catch a mega-bozo in action in a public bathroom, copying down the phone numbers of "fast" women. Even rarer is a glimpse of a terminal bozo coming out of the bozoettes' room after he's written his **own** name and phone number on the wall.

Certain places are packed with specific types of bozos. A Judas Priest concert, for example, will be filled with Party Animal bozos. Similarly, most over-priced racquetball clubs are teeming with Too-Hip-Mid-Life Crisis bozos.

But if you want to see bozos in action without leaving your house, switch on a rerun of "Gilligan's Island."

The Most Popular Careers for Mega-bozos

1. Professional blood donor
2. Mud wrestler
3. Nielsen family

3
Classic Bozotypes

If there are billions of bozos, then there are just as many differences and variations among them. But certain patterns and attributes are repeated over and over again.

Throughout the remainder of this book you will find depictions of some classic bozotypes. Some inter-bozotype variations exist, so not *all* Garden Variety Working Bozos will appear exactly as shown, but these illustrations serve as a good field guide for further study and observation.

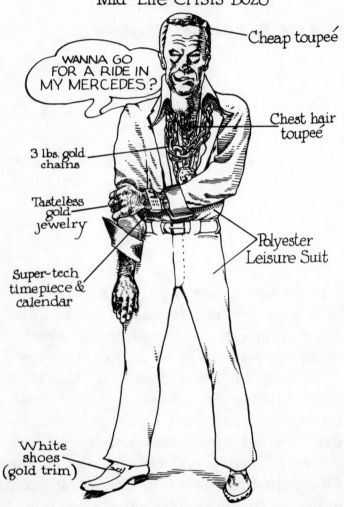

4
In Search of Famous Bozos

What about famous people—celebrities, actors, sports stars, etc. Are there many famous bozos? Will the weatherman screw up the forecast this weekend when you make plans to go to the beach?

Of *course* there are famous bozos.

Some people are universally recognized as bozos, so let's begin with them, to get an idea of what the mega-bozo end of the spectrum looks like.

Anyone who makes his or her living as a bozo or bozoette is a mega-bozo. Famous mega-bozos include Richard Simmons, Howard Cosell and Liberace. The reigning mega-bozo in the children's division is Mister Rogers, who still speaks as if his brain is not connected to his lips.

Your basic garden variety famous bozo is found everywhere you look on television. Recent studies show you can spot an average of 3.7 bozos during every minute of viewing.

What separates the average bozo from the bozo who thinks he isn't one is bozo consciousness. The bozo who is but thinks he isn't gets a few points for trying—at least he's aware enough to know that there is such a thing as a bozo. It just hasn't occurred to him that he is one.

For example, Billy Martin gets the benefit of the doubt. He's a bozo, but he thinks he's not. Woody Hayes, on the other hand, has no conception of bozoity. He's a megabozo candidate.

Hugh Hefner thinks he's just about the hippest person in the galaxy, but you have to wonder about a guy who spends his whole life in his pajamas.

None of the Beatles were bozos. Elton John is. Many rock stars tend to be a bit bozoic without knowing it. A prime example is Jerry Garcia, lead guitarist for the Grateful Dead. He was stuck in a time warp in 1966, and will probably never get out.

Some people are bozos for parts of their lives, and nonbozos during others. Timing is very important here.

George Plimpton, the writer, was a non-bozo.

George Plimpton, the Intellivision spokes-man and television personality, is a bozo.

Some people can live their entire lives as non-bozos, then lose it, and do incredibly bozoic things. Richard Pryor is a good example. He's certainly a non-bozo, but setting yourself on fire is *real* bozoic. Fortunately, he has returned to the ranks of the non-bozos, largely because he recognizes a bozo move when he makes one, and sees the humor in it.

John DeLorean is a similar case. He gets the "No Bozos" Special Award for the Best Single Bozoic Event in the Life of a Non-Bozo. (Cheer up, John. Even if you end up making license plates, you'll still be in the car business, right?)

Famous Bozos

Pat Boone
Anita Bryant
Billy Carter
Boy George
Joanna Carson
Jerry Falwell
Gerald Ford
Elmer Fudd
Rita Jenrette
Ayatollah Khomeini
Barry Manilow
Reverend Sun Yung Moon
Madalyn Murray-O'Hair
Brent Musburger
Phyllis Schafly
George Steinbrenner
James Watt

Bozos Who Think They're Not

Muhammad Ali

David Brenner

Dr. Joyce Brothers

Chevy Chase (almost reaches megabozo status with each new pratfall)

Angie Dickinson

Joe DiMaggio (as Mr. Coffee)

Erik Estrada

J.R. Ewing

Farrah Fawcett

Sigmund Freud

Charlton Heston

Evel Knievel

Billy Martin

Professional football cheerleaders

Geraldo Rivera

Telly Savalas

Gloria Vanderbilt

Andy Warhol

Famous Non-Bozos

Alan Alda

Woody Allen

Humphrey Bogart

Lloyd Bridges

Bugs Bunny

George Burns

Ray Charles

Sean Connery

Walter Cronkite

James Dean

Robert De Niro

Joe DiMaggio (as Mr. Baseball)

E.T.

God

Lee Iaccoca

Reggie Jackson

Martin Luther King

Paul Newman

Jack Nicholson
Miss Piggy
Monty Python (collectively and individually)
Robert Redford
Tom Robbins
Bruce Springsteen
Garry Trudeau
Mae West
Stevie Wonder

Almost Bozos

John Anderson
Dick Cavett
Steve Garvey
Bob Hope
Kermit the Frog
Don Meredith
Nancy Reagan
Ted Turner

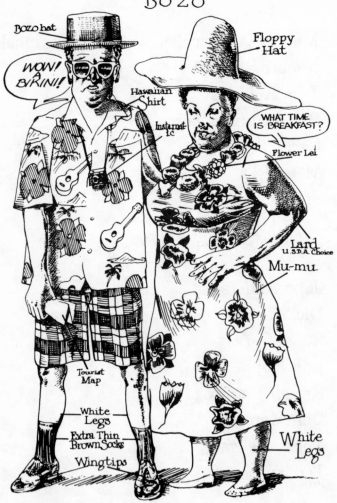

Bozo/Bozoette Couples

Donnie and Marie Osmond
Sonny and Cher
Wayland and Madame
John and Bo Derek
Elizabeth Taylor and anyone
Lenny and Squiggy
Tiny Tim and Miss Vicki
Steve Lawrence and Eydie Gorme
   (Hall of Fame Charter Members)
Xavier Cugat and Charo
Prince Andrew and Koo Stark
Marvin Hamlisch and Cyndy Garvey

Non-Bozo/Bozoette Couples

Fred Astaire and Ginger Rogers
Harry and Bess Truman
Orville and Wilbur Wright
peanut butter (chunky) and jelly

5
Fads and Fashion

One of the reasons bozos are bozos is that they simply refuse to get with the program. No matter what, they always seem to be a beat behind the rest of the band. (This bozoic metaphor is quite literally why so few bozos make it as professional drummers.)

This lack of timing, coupled with another unfortunate trait of most bozos—their tendency to be followers rather than leaders—helps explains why non-bozos create trends, and bozos fuel fads.

Let's say some non-bozo is fiddling around in his garage, and comes up with a new kind of lamp. He puts this plastic stuff inside a container along with some water, and has the light bulb heat up the plastic. The plastic rises in the container as it gets hot, and bubbles up to the surface.

Presto! The lava lamp is born!

The first 150 people who buy the lava lamp in a little specialty store have a pretty nice conversation piece. It's new and different, and is a pretty good way to get a girl to come up to your apartment if you don't have any etchings.

But then bozos find out about it. Suddenly, lava lamps are being mass-produced, and every trinket store in the known world is selling them for $29.95. Bozos and bozoettes flood the stores to buy their very own.

As soon as that happened, non-bozos trashed their lava lamps, and moved on to something else. But in many towns today, bozos and bozoettes still turn on their lava lamps when "company" comes over.

OK. Maybe lava lamps weren't a great example, since they were bozoic from the beginning. But the principle applies to almost everything that goes through the trend/fad cycle.

Pac-Man was a great video game, until

bozos got hold of it. For a while, you couldn't leave the house without seeing something with Pac-Man on it. Coffee mugs, placemats, bumper stickers, t-shirts, cereal, notebooks, underwear (!!!)—you name it. Fortunately, even bozos have limits, and the Pac-Man telephone was a real flop.

Timing is only part of the picture, though. Bozos don't know when to quit. Once they decide they like something, its importance to their lives grows all out of proportion, so they don't want to let go of it.

"Star Trek" bozos are a good example. Most non-bozos occasionally enjoy a rerun of "Star Trek," and recognize that it was pretty good entertainment. A "Star Trek" junkie, however, has seen every episode at least five times, can recite them, knows all characters, villains and plot lines, and is convinced that life on Earth will end the day "Star Trek" no longer appears on television. These people even have "Star Trek" parties in which they dress up as characters from the show.

"Star Trek" junkies, being serious bozos

and bozoettes, are also likely to have bean bag chairs in their living rooms, which they still consider fashionable and useful furniture.

Using the principles of lack of timing and excess, it's easy to spot bozos and bozoettes in daily life.

Look! There's one now! He's the guy at the ice cream store wearing the running suit, slurping a triple-scoop of the disgusting new flavor of the month. By the looks of his belly, the last time he ran anywhere was in junior high when a big kid was chasing him.

There's a bozoette over at the beauty parlor, getting her hair teased and sprayed. Earl Scheib could have picked a better color.

Don't look now, but a bozo in the phone booth just checked the slot for a forgotten dime. Yeah, that's him—the one in the Nehru jacket.

You get the idea.

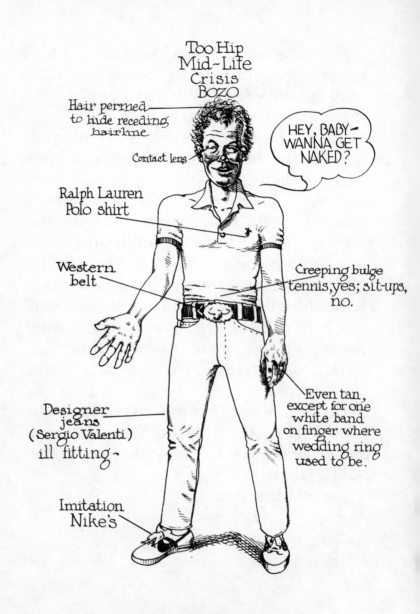

6
Places Bozos Go and Things Bozos Do On Vacation

1. Tijuana, to see real Mexicans and buy plaster casts of animals which glow in the dark.

2. The Poconos, for a bozo honeymoon. (In California, they go to the Madonna Inn.)

3. A Hostess bakery, for a tour on "half-price" day.

4. Grauman's Chinese Theatre in Hollywood, to put their hands in the cement prints of dead movie stars.

5. Any meteor crater in the desert.

6. Stay at home and think about work.

7. Mom's house, to get a free meal.

8. The airport, to watch the planes and pretend they're going somewhere.

7
Bozos in Motion

Besides their wardrobes, perhaps nothing identifies the modern bozo and bozoette quite like the way they conduct themselves on the highways of life. You can instantly spot a potential bozo by the car he drives, and the way he drives it.

● Bozos always leave their turn signals on, miles after they have changed lanes.

● Bozos like to stop for yellow lights, especially if they are in front of you.

● At a four-way stop sign, they never seem to know when it's their turn to go, and screw up the flow of traffic through the intersection.

● If your state allows a right turn on a red

light, you can bet the bozo in front of you will hog the right lane, and then go straight when the light changes to green.

● Bozos in front of you always drive five miles per hour slower than you want to go.

● Bozos behind you always want to drive five miles per hour faster than you want to.

● When entering a freeway or turnpike, you can easily spot the bozo—he's the one stopped on the on ramp. For some reason, bozos don't know how to "merge." Sometimes it takes a bozo all day just to get on the freeway.

● Bozos park half an inch from your rear bumper, even if it's a mile to the next car behind them.

● Bozos who drive big American cars with gas nozzles located under the rear license plate always seem to misplace their gas caps. When they accelerate from stop lights, they leave a trail of gas. Then they wonder why their land yachts get only three miles to the gallon.

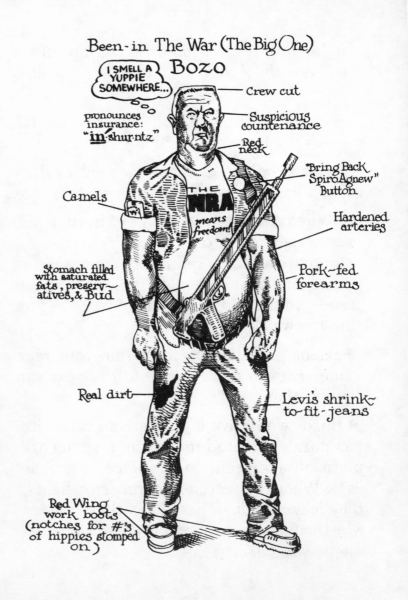

● Bozos throw trash out their car windows.

● When a bozo gets into a strange car, he runs his hand along the crack in the back seat, hoping to find lost change.

● Bozos like to entertain themselves by singing along with their car radios—loudly and off key.

● Bozos have bumperstickers which read "I ♥ my..." followed by drawings of their bozo pets. Other popular bozo bumperstickers begin with "I ♥," followed by the names of places other than where they are.

● Bozos (and especially bozoettes) like those little bobbing head dolls, which they put on the rear shelves of their cars, so the little figures will nod at you all the way down the street. Bozos also like to affix waving hands to the side windows of their Ford Falcons.

● Bozos put fake fur on the dashboard. They also hang things from the rear view mirror—little stuffed animals, mango-scented car deodorizers and dice.

- Horns that play the first notes of a song or mimic a cattle call are *très* bozoic.

- Bozos love to buy used police cars (that haven't been repainted) and drive around trying to look tough.

- You can spot bozos wandering around in shopping center parking lots, especially during Christmas season. They park their bozomobiles, walk into the mall, and hours later have forgotten where they parked.

- Bozos love drive-up windows of all kinds. In fact, they'll make special trips to fast food restaurants, banks, and convenience stores just to use a drive-up window. They feel safe and important in their cars, and would rather talk to a machine than a person. Of course, they say things like "Roger" and "You copy that?" into the speaker.

- On airplanes, bozos always sit next to the window, and want to get up every fifteen minutes to go to the bathroom.

- They always bug the stewardesses.

(Now they're called flight attendants, but bozos still call them stewardesses.) Bozos are the reason flight attendants make so much money.

● If you want to sleep on an airplane, the bozo sitting next to you will talk constantly about his family, and have 280 out-of-focus photos in his wallet that he insists you examine closely.

● When the bozo next to you finally falls asleep, he will:
1. drool.
2. snore.
3. rest his head on your shoulder.

Bozo Cars

AMC Gremlin

AMC Matador

AMC Pacer

Cadillac Eldorado

Chevrolet Chevette

Chevrolet Vega

Chrysler Cordoba

Dodge Dart (1970 or earlier)

Ford Falcon

Ford Granada

Ford Maverick

Ford Mustang (1969-1981)

Ford Pinto (especially if it's been "souped up")

Lincoln Continental

Mercedes Benz diesel (when driven by a thrifty bozo)

Mercedes Benz 450 SL (when driven by a Mid-Life Crisis bozo)

Oldsmobile Cutlass (#1 bozo car in America)

Winnebago (mega-bozo status is achieved if back window has decals from more than 20 states)

Any car the size of Delaware

4-wheel drive pickup truck (when driven in the city) (possible mega-bozo status if there is a German shepherd in the back)

Non-Bozo Cars

BMW (1600, 2002 tii, 3.0 csi only)

Chrysler LeBaron convertible

Ferrari

Ford Mustang (1965-66, 1982-4)

Ford T-Bird (1955-59)

Honda (Prelude 1984, CRX 1984 only)

Jaguar

Karmann Ghia

Peugeot (403, 505, 604 only)

Porsche

Rolls Royce

Saab

Volvo (pre-1969 only)

VW Van

Cars that go Both Ways

Audi

Chevrolet Camaro

Chevrolet Corvair

Chevrolet Corvette

Chrysler K-cars

Datsun 280Z (It's a bozo car if it has a
   personalized license plate with a "Z" in
   it.)

DeLorean

Jeep

Mercedes Benz

Pontiac Firebird

8
Bozos in History

Most Bozologists now agree that bozos have existed as long as mankind itself. This would explain why recorded history is really nothing more than 25 years of events, repeated again and again by different bozos in a variety of locations.

But bozoity might go back even further. One theory traces bozoity back to the day the continents began to drift apart. The end result—seven continents instead of a single convenient one—did nothing except increase long-distance phone rates and strand most of the funny-looking animals in Australia.

Dr. Bozotros is among those who believe that bozoity began with mankind. He believes that there have always been bozos among us, but that they have never been as common as today. For some as yet unexplained reason, the number of bozos increased rapidly with the advent of TV dinners, jockey shorts and Minute Rice.

Even though it's difficult to separate "bozo history" from "non-bozo history" (especially lately), what follows are some highlights of past bozo events.

A sampling of bozoic historical events

1 million B.C—Non-bozo Adam bites the apple, becomes first bozo.

1500 B.C.—First modern calendar built at Stonehenge. It is found to be too big to be practical.

300 B.C.—Chinese refuse to communicate with their neighbors, who look and talk funny. They build the Great Wall to keep the bozos out.

725 A.D.—First mechanical clock built in China. Shortly thereafter, the concept of "being late" begins to catch on among bozos.

1200—The Crusades prove that bozos will flock to miserable, faraway places if allowed to travel with large groups of fellow bozos and bozoettes. Beginning of tours and tour groups.

1256—Gunpowder invented. Proves to be the first step in a more efficient way for bozos to kill each other.

1626—Sir Francis Bacon (a non-bozo all his life) dies from a bozo stunt. To test his concept of freezing food, he packs a dead fowl with snow. He dies of exposure just after reporting the success of the experiment.

1684—Issac Newton discovers gravity. Bozos in China are especially grateful, since they can now walk freely on the planet with no fear of falling off.

1770—First great American bozo idea. The art of "tarring and feathering" invented in Salem, Massachusetts.

1773—Another bozo experiment by a non-bozo. Benjamin Franklin electrocutes chickens, turkeys, and a lamb.

1775—Austrian physician Franz Mesmer uses his "animal magnetism" to cure hysterical patients. Later, he elopes with a cow who has fallen madly in love with him.

1820—Twenty-five bozos in Congress vote to support a fund for Captain John Symmes' search for life inside this "hollow" planet. Later, when

Symmes goes ahead with his plan (without any government money) he finds an incredible civilization of worms, ants, and moles.

1833—George Fibbleton (his real name) invents a shaving machine. A true bozo device, it shaves off more skin than beard, and is not a tremendous success.

1837—P.T. Barnum, perhaps the world's first bozologist, creates his first successful hoax. Ten thousand New Yorkers pay to see Joice Heth, a 46-pound, 161 year-old slave who supposedly brought George Washington into the world.

1843—A Troy, Ohio man is fined $10 for kissing a married lady. To test the bozo ordinance, he asks the court how much he'd have to pay for "the works," and is promptly thrown in jail for contempt.

1867—Bozo Russians sell Alaska to U.S. for less than 2¢ an acre.

1883—Brooklyn Bridge completed. The next day, an unidentified man becomes the first bozo to buy it.

April 19, 1910—Halley's comet appears. As usual, bozos expect the worst. As usual, worst doesn't happen.

1921—Betty Crocker "born." Actually, Betty is created by an advertising executive. But that doesn't keep bozoettes from making the Betty Crocker Cookbook the best-selling non-fiction book in 1950.

1934—Muzak invented.

1935—Carl C. Magee invents the parking meter. First bozo city to install them—Oklahoma City, Oklahoma.

1943—Pentagon building completed at a cost of $83 billion. It's the world's largest building in area, and houses the world's largest concentration of bozos.

Nov. 3, 1948—Chicago *Tribune* headline declares Thomas Dewey victor over Harry Truman in Presidential election.

1952—Americans spend $135 million on the more than 90 "deodorizing" products which contain chlorophyll. The fad quickly dies after "The Journal of the American Medical Association" points out that grazing goats live on chlorophyll, and still smell horrible.

1952—First 3-D movie, "Bwana Devil," opens in Los Angeles. Proves that bozos will pay hard-earned cash to sit in the dark and wear funny glasses.

1952—Palmer Paint Company of Detroit invents the paint-by-numbers kit. One paint-by-numbers artist is awarded 3rd prize by unsuspecting judges at a San Francisco art show.

1954—Mega-bozos in advertising attempt the world's dumbest comparison: "The bomb's (hydrogen) brilliant gleam reminds me of the brilliant gleam Beacon Wax gives to floors. It's a science marvel!" read an ad in the Pittsburgh *Press*.

Feb. 1971—Richard M. Nixon, by then a certified mega-bozo, installs tape recording equipment in the Oval Office, so the decisions made during his Presidency can be recorded for posterity. They are.

1974—When Taiwanese teams embarrass American kids once too often in the Little League World Series, American bozos band together and do the logical bozo thing: Non-U.S. teams are banned from further play.

1977—Kellogg's reduces the iron content of its Frosted Rice cereal after consumers discovered they could move flakes of the cereal around with a magnet.

1979—Marc Quiquandon, world's record holder for snail eating, dies after eating 72 in three minutes.

1982—Bozo hijacker at Los Angeles International Airport opens emergency door because the plane is too warm. Non-bozo passenger pushes him out onto the runway, 30 feet below.

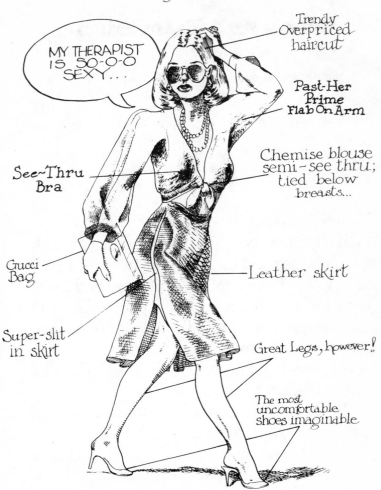

9
Bozos and Television

Sincerity is the quality that comes through on television.
—Richard Nixon, bozo, 1955

Television is a triumph of equipment over people, and
the minds that control it are so small that you could put
them in the navel of a flea and still have enough room
beside them for a network vice-president's heart.
—Fred Allen, non-bozo

Television is, quite simply, the showcase for
modern bozoity. It is the window through
which most bozos view the world. From
television, bozos see what is new and fashionable, so the medium is probably the
greatest single source for all that is bozoic.

TV didn't have to become a tool of the
bozo, but it came of age in the 50's (The
Bozo Decade).

In the beginning, television was fresh and
unpredictable, which gave it genuine charm.
"Uncle Milty" Berle didn't mind making a
fool of himself, and his bozo audience loved
it. Non-bozos such as Sid Caesar and

Imogene Coca brought social satire to the living rooms of America, deftly crossing back and forth over the bozo line to appeal to bozos and non-bozos alike.

Ironically, it was television genius Desi Arnaz who helped seal the fate of TV as the mouthpiece of bozoity. He got the bright idea to film each episode of "I Love Lucy" as it was being performed for an audience. Without knowing it at the time, he invented the rerun, and changed the face of TV forever.

Thanks a lot, Desi.

Filmed shows allowed the opportunity to do a scene again if it wasn't perfect, or if the audience didn't laugh in the right places. Then some bozo realized that they didn't need to film the shows in front of a live audience at all—it would be cheaper and easier if they faked an audience response.* With the invention of canned laughter, TV officially became the Land of the Bozos.

---

*Unfortunately, the bozoic logic ended there, short of the next step, which would have recognized the superfluity of showing the product to any real audience at all.

Scheduled programming is only part of the story, because advertisers recognized the potential of TV immediately. Imagine, millions of bozos watching the same program! What better way to sell the vital things of life—floor wax, cigarettes, dish soap that smells like limes, dog food, and (of course) TV dinners.

So where is the non-bozoic material on television? Hidden like half-carat diamonds in Mount Bandini, that's where. Most of the non-bozo shows like "60 Minutes" have been around for years. Even the evening news, long the stalwart of non-bozo TV, is now so riddled with show-biz bozos that it's hard to believe that Uncle Walter Cronkite retired just a couple of years ago to become Mr. Wizard.

But not to worry! The average bozo and bozoette loves television, and could watch soap operas and game shows until their eyeballs glaze over.

If the rest of the country recycled its trash like television does, nothing in America would ever be wasted.

Shows that Prove TV
is Designed for Bozos

Laverne and Shirley

Dukes of Hazzard

Hee Haw

That's Incredible/Real People

Alice

CHiPs

Family Feud

Lawrence Welk Show

Hall of Fame Members

My Mother the Car

Gilligan's Island

Girl from U.N.C.L.E.

The Beverly Hillbillies

Love American Style

The Munsters

Twenty-One (the king of the fixed quiz shows of the 50's)

TV Shows that Prove Even Bozos Can Do Things Right—Sometimes

Leave it to Beaver
Twilight Zone
The Honeymooners
Get Smart
The Dick Van Dyke Show
Bonanza
Rocky and Bullwinkle
I Love Lucy
Father Knows Best
Hogan's Heroes
Star Trek
Playhouse 90
The Carol Burnett Show

Honorable Mention

The Lone Ranger

Alfred Hitchcock Presents

Rawhide

The Jetsons

The Flintstones

The Wonderful World of Disney

Make Room for Daddy

Dobie Gillis

See It Now

Sea Hunt

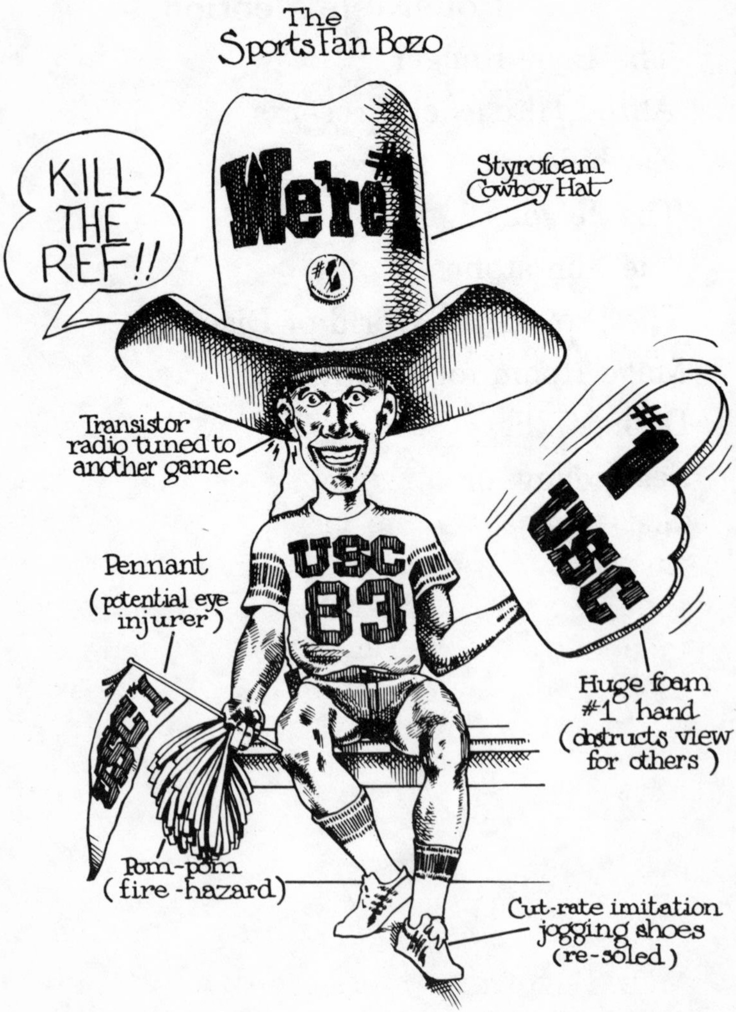
The Sports Fan Bozo
KILL THE REF!!
We're #1
Styrofoam Cowboy Hat
Transistor radio tuned to another game.
USC 83
#1 USC
Pennant (potential eye injurer)
USC #1
Huge foam #1 hand (obstructs view for others)
Pom-pom (fire-hazard)
Cut-rate imitation jogging shoes (re-soled)

10
The Bozotros Scale

One outgrowth of Dr. Bozotros' studies of bozology is his 10-point scale of bozoity. This scale measures the amount of bozoity in a person or thing, much like the Richter Scale measures the intensity of an earthquake. Unlike the Richter Scale, however, the Bozotros Scale is center-weighted, which means that a score of five is neutral—neither bozoic nor non-bozoic. Here's what the scale looks like:

0	1	2	3	4	5	6	7	8	9	10

Free of bozoity
(strictly a theo-
retical value)

Bozo
balanced

Mega-
bozo
territory

Dr. Bozotros prefers to use his 10-point bozo scale to rate inanimate objects and situations or events rather than people. "People are harder to rate, because a non-bozo is apt to do several bozoic things in the course of a day," said Dr. Bozotros. "So I rate people as *bozos*, *almost bozos*, and *non-bozos* most of the time, and use the Bozo Scale to give more detailed ratings on bozoic things—Cheez Whiz, octopi made out of yarn—those kinds of things."

The following list of random items evaluated on the 10-point Bozotros Scale will give you, the bozo watcher, a good idea of its usefulness in everyday life.

Examples of the Bozotros Scale in Action

Item	Rating	Comments
Designer underwear	7	Just who are they trying to impress, anyway?
Whoopie cushions	10	Mega-bozo territory
Political campaign commercials	9	Thank God elections only happen every two years.
Health foods (in realistic quantities)	3	
(with unremitting regularity)	7	A sign of a "new age" bozo

Running shoes		
(when used for running)	2	A great idea
(when used for "image")	8	Bozoville
Hawaiian-style pizza	6	Pineapple on a pizza? Who thought of that?
Plastic flowers	9	No redeeming value
Twinkies (also Ding-Dongs, and other alternative food)	8	A good argument for a total health food diet.
Whisky decanters in the shape of cars, animals, and dead rock 'n' roll stars	10	Who buys these things?
Sea monkeys	6	OK as a one-shot gift for a kid.
Starch blockers	8	Only a bozo would believe this one.
Any record album by Ronco or K-TEL	7	Save your money, listen to the radio instead.
Waterbeds	3	Those who like them speak well of them.
Carpets depicting dogs playing cards	8	Bozos will buy anything.
CB radios	7	Passé
Using CB jargon	10	10-4, big buddy. Got a mega-bozo here.
Bowling	5	Neutral—but why do so many bozos bowl?

Houseplants	2	A great idea, as long as you remember to water.
Nose plugs for swimming	7	May serve a useful function, but really looks bozoic.
"Cat's eye" glasses (c. 1957)	9	Get with it, bozoette.
Velvet portraits of Elvis	9	Tacky, very tacky.
Subscription to the National Enquirer	10	Mega-bozoette
Mirrored sunglasses	5	Had their day. Future bozo item.
Scotch Tape	1	One of the truly great little inventions of all time.
Leopard-print anything	8	Pretty dumb attire in a city or suburb when you think about it.
Rubik's cube keychains	7	Who the hell is Rubik, anyway?
Spam	10	One of the first mega-bozo inventions.
Presto logs	8	Coming soon: logs pressed from dried road apples!
Monosodium glutamate	9	Drugs for your tongue
Backpack blowers, used to "sweep" sidewalks	7	Only slightly better than using 5 million gallons of water to do the same thing.

Fruitcake	8	Use it as a doorstop.
Fresno, California	8	Lots of bozos here, folks.
Digital wrist watches that play music	9	Why do the alarms on these watches always go off during the quiet part of the symphony or the movie?
Anything for the home bar that lights up with a "Bar is Open" message	10	Welcome home, mega-bozo.
Imitation margarine	10+	Beyond bozoity

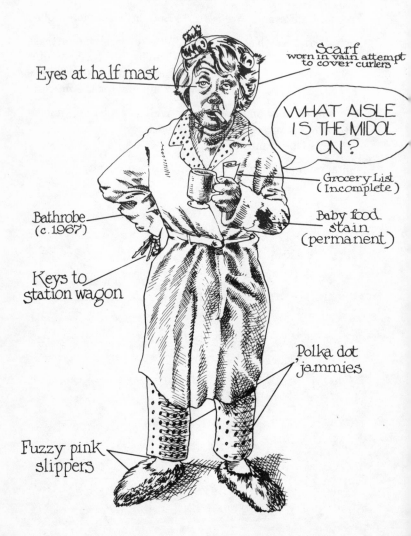

11
Bozo Goes to the Movies

Unlike sporting events, where bozoic behavior such as yelling "You make your mama sick, lizard face!", second-guessing the coaches, and spilling beer down people's backs is perfectly acceptable, a movie theatre demands strict non-bozo compliance. Because of this, bozoic behavior at the movies is especially obvious and annoying.

Whenever a non-bozo goes to the movies, a bozo with a popcorn the size of a trash dumpster will sit directly behind him and munch his way through all the best scenes.

When you finally get fed up enough to move to another seat, the floor beneath you will be incredibly sticky from the Coke spilled by the last bozo to sit there.

In a crowded theatre, the average non-bozo will inevitably sit near a mega-bozo, who will make loud, bozoic comments.

If you get to the theatre late, the only seat left will be directly behind the biggest bozo in the place. We're talking six feet, nine inches, 300 pounds, body odor, and possibly a large cowboy hat. With any luck, he'll leave to get popcorn and you'll see ten or fifteen minutes of the film (but none of the good parts).

Ten Things that Bozos Worry About

1. body odor
2. dirty underwear
3. bad breath
4. loose dentures
5. ring around the collar
6. being popular
7. split ends
8. irregularity
9. warts
10. dandruff

12
How to Get Rid of a Bozo

High in the mountains of Asia, nestled between China and India, lies a little-known country called Bhutan. Few people have ever heard of it, because it maintains no contact with the outside world, and its borders are closed to all travellers. But every serious bozologist knows plenty about this remote little country, because it is absolutely bozo-free.

In the most sacred room of the largest and oldest temple in Bhutan, hangs an ancient hand-woven tapestry. Several years ago, when the King of Bhutan opened the country's borders for a few select Western tourists, several Bozologists were among the first outsiders to enter the holy shrine, and read the great words of wisdom which are woven into it, Those who viewed the historic tapestry were sworn to secrecy, but one astute bozologist, knowing that the King was a fanatical basketball fan, bribed him with a championship ball autographed by the 1972 Los Angeles Lakers.* We are indebted to this bozologist for bringing back the words inscribed on the great tapestry.

Here is what is written:

How to Get Rid of a Bozo

1. Tell him there's a close-out sale on bermuda shorts at K-Mart.

2. Give him the name and address of someone who owns every K-TEL record.

3. Give him a quarter and point him in the direction of the nearest video game.

4. Play hide and seek, and skip the "seek" part.

5. Talk intelligently to him about a subject of great world importance.

*Well, maybe there is a bozo in Bhutan, after all.

6. Tell him a meter maid is about to ticket his car. He will dash to the street, whether or not he has a car.

7. Hide his wing-tips.

8. Tell him Liberace is across the street.

9. Tell him the polyester fabric factory gives free tours, and if he hurries he can still make it.

13
The Bozo Test

Take this test to find out how big a bozo you are.

TRUE/FALSE:

1. Dear Abby should be President.

2. I have read the National Enquirer. (Standing in line in the supermarket counts, too).

3. I never take stupid tests like this one.

4. I am not a bozo.

5. It ruins my day when I come home and the phone is ringing and I run in the door but the guy on the other end hangs up and I can't figure out who was calling.

MULTIPLE CHOICE:

6. When you hear the word "bozo," what's the first thing you think of?

  a. a clown

  b. Merv Griffin

  c. your boss

  d. yourself

7. Which of the following would you rather do?

  a. watch the neighbors' windows with binoculars

  b. spend an entire afternoon watching game shows and eating junk food

  c. figure out the odds of your getting a date with Brooke Shields

  d. try to find out why you can't sneeze with your eyes open

8. The nose_____.

  a. knows

  b. blows

  c. snows

  d. runs

9. Which of the following do you find most amusing?

    a. designer underwear

    b. deodorant underwear

    c. invisible underwear

    d. James Under, inventor of underwear

10. Which of the following do you find least amusing?

    a. nuclear-powered dentures

    b. nose hair

    c. meat thermometers

    d. Liberace

11. Which of these comes closest to your goals in life?

    a. a charming wife, 2⅓ children, a heavily mortgaged house in suburbia, a 25" color TV, a shaggy but lovable dog, and a Winnebago

    b. a good-paying job

    c. a job, any job

    d. the keys to every donut shop in the state

12. Your house is burning down, and you only have

Party Animal Bozo

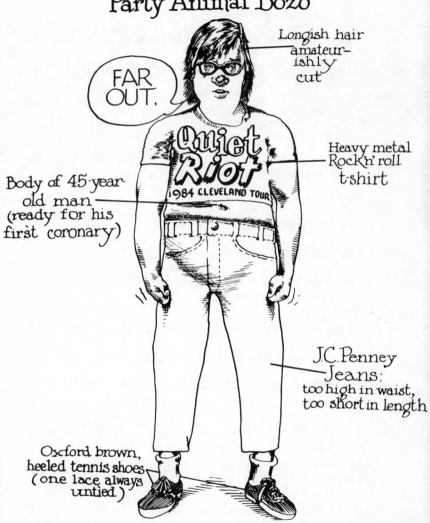

time to save one thing. Which of the following would you save?

a. your white loafers and matching white belt

b. the lemon-yellow leisure suit you bought on sale at Sears.

c. your checkbook

d. the keys to every donut shop in the state

13. The best things in life are _____.

a. free

b. too damn expensive

c. fattening

d. bound to cause cancer, blindness, and eternal damnation

14. The term "bozo consciousness" refers to

a. a freshman psychology class

b. the realization that after 25 years of hard work all you get is a gold watch

c. the ability to tell a red rubber nose from a suitcase full of inflatable shoes

d. a clown waking up in the morning who thinks his waterbed has sprung a leak, only he doesn't have a waterbed

15. You are the personnel manager for a small but thriving business. There are two applicants for one job opening. One of them has a crew cut, shiny wing-tips, and Sen-Sen breath. The other has purple spiked hair and a tattoo on his cheek. You would:

   a. hire the crew cut

   b. carefully weigh the talents and abilities of each, and then hire the crew cut because nobody weird is going to work for you

   c. hire the crew cut because you can't believe how shiny his wing-tips are

   d. hire the punk because he's your son

16. You know a guy or girl who is a real bozo/bozo-ette because he/she

   a. was President of the Chess Club in high school

   b. thought the "rhythm method" was a correspondence course for drummers

   c. ate Twinkies and loved them

   d. never liked me after I flew his/her underwear on the flagpole

17. When trying to catch a bozo, the best bait to use is:

    a. two tickets to a Wayne Newton show

    b. a 3-D poster of Dolly Parton

    c. a certificate good for a weekend for two in Burbank

    d. a 1963 Fairlane station wagon with the keys in the ignition and a six-pack of Brew 102 on the front seat

18. You are taking this test because

    a. you know you're not a bozo, but you want to make sure

    b. you suspect a friend of yours is a bozo and you want to know what to look for

    c. you're a sucker for stupid quizzes

    d. you're sick and tired of people calling you a bozo and laughing at you behind your back. In fact, the next idiot who calls you a bozo is going to get an imprint of your Elk's Club ring right in the middle of his nose

SCORING THE TEST: Give yourself five points for every question you answered True, three points for every False. You get one point for every "a," two points for each "b," three points for every "c" answer, and six-and-a-half points for every "d." Add to this the number of questions you had to guess the answer. Then add to this total your age in five years and your hat size (to the nearest 1/8th). Subtract from this total the number of days since you last had sex. Divide this total by two, and add the number of truly great pizzas you've had in your entire lifetime. You now have your Bozoscore.

INTERPRETING YOUR SCORE: If you didn't take the test, you pass. If you took the test and wrote down your answers as you went along, you're a bozo. If you went through the entire scoring process, you are a mega-bozo.

14
You REALLY Know You're a Bozo When . . .

1. The sales clerks at Woolworth's know your first name.

2. No matter where you go, someone laughs when you walk into a room.

3. None of your computer dates will speak to you.

4. TV dinners actually taste good.

5. The thought of a public toilet seat makes you break out in a rash.

6. You still think it's hip to have a decal of Woody Woodpecker on your car.

7. You buy your clothes at the supermarket.

8. You plan your day around the reruns of "My Mother the Car" and "Petticoat Junction."

9. You defend vinyl clothes as practical and stylish.

10. The only restaurants you go to have drive-up windows.

11. You wake up after your wedding night with your clothes on.

12. People look at the length of your pants legs and ask if you're grown lately.

13. In your best "cool" imitation, you pretend to smoke a cigarette, but don't know which end to light.

14. You never understand jokes, even after three people explain them to you.

15. You look forward to your junk mail.

16. You walk around all morning with toilet paper stuck to the bottom of your shoe, and nobody notices anything different about you.

17. Your dog barks at you every time you come home.

18. Your boss gives everyone the day off except you.

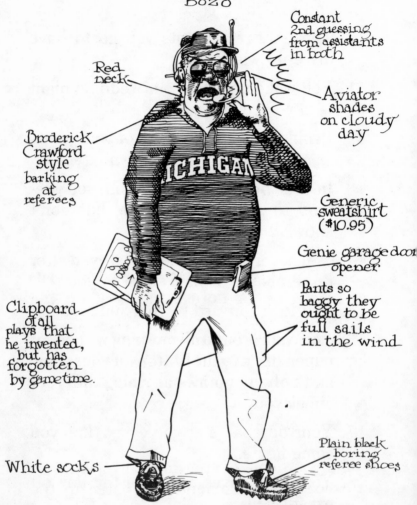

American Football Coach
Bozo

Constant 2nd guessing from assistants in booth

Red neck

Aviator shades on cloudy day

Broderick Crawford style barking at referees

ICHIGAN

Generic sweatshirt ($10.95)

Genie garage door opener

Pants so baggy they ought to be full sails in the wind

Clipboard of all plays that he invented, but has forgotten by gametime.

White socks

Plain black boring referee shoes

15
The End/The Beginning

Congratulations. After reading this book, you now know more about bozos than most bozos know about themselves. You are now fully able to function in a world crawling with bozos and mega-bozos.

You know what they look like, and how they act.

You know what they do, where they do it, and even the kind of car they'll be driving home afterwards.

But most importantly, you know how to keep them out of your life—and keep yourself from becoming a bozo as well.

Now that you're a serious amateur Bozologist, continue to watch for bozos wherever you go.

As you delve deeper into the science of bozology, I recommend you listen to the record album that started it all, "I Think

We're All Bozos on This Bus," by the Firesign Theatre. It is a bizarre look at bozos in the past, present, and future, and is required listening for anyone who wishes to become a doctor of bozology.

Whatever else happens, always remember that bozoity is a *curable* condition. If you're a bozo now, you *can* become a regular, normal person—if you want to be. And your bozo loved ones *can* be helped. All it takes is time, patience, and some non-bozo conditioning.

But it may not be easy—living with bozos is *seldom* easy. To paraphrase the "Bozos" album, living in this world full of bozos is a little like having bees live in your head.

But, there they are.

So do your part as a non-bozo to help rid the world of bozoity, and maybe our kids can inherit a world with no war, no famine, no drugs, no polyester, no plastic potted plants, no Beverly Hills Diet, no Helen Reddy, no Pringle's potato chips, no "light" beer—and no bozos.

The End.